# DREAM BIG,
## STAY POSITIVE,
### AND
## BELIEVE IN
# YOURSELF

D0027272

# Blue Mountain Arts®

*New and Best-Selling Titles*

**By Susan Polis Schutz:**

*To My Daughter with Love
on the Important Things in Life*

*To My Grandchild with Love*

*To My Son with Love*

**By Douglas Pagels:**

*Always Remember How Special
You Are to Me*

*For You, My Soul Mate*

*The Next Chapter of Your Life*

*Required Reading for All Teenagers*

*Simple Thoughts That Can Literally
Change Your Life*

*You Are One Amazing Lady*

**By Wally Amos, with Stu Glauberman:**

*The Path to Success Is Paved
with Positive Thinking*

**By Debra DiPietro:**

*Short Morning Prayers*

**By Marci:**

*Angels Are Everywhere!*

*Friends Are Forever*

*10 Simple Things to Remember*

*To My Daughter*

*To My Granddaughter*

*To My Mother*

*To My Sister*

*To My Son*

*You Are My "Once in a Lifetime"*

**By Minx Boren:**

*Friendship Is a Journey*

*Healing Is a Journey*

**By Carol Wiseman:**

*Emerging from the Heartache of Loss*

**By Latesha Randall,
with Sebastian Walter:**

*The To-Be List*

**Anthologies:**

*A Daybook of Positive Thinking*

*A Son Is Life's Greatest Gift*

*Dream Big, Stay Positive, and Believe in Yourself*

*Girlfriends Are the Best Friends of All*

*God Is Always Watching Over You*

*Hang In There*

*The Love Between a Mother and Daughter Is Forever*

*Nothing Fills the Heart with Joy like a Grandson*

*There Is Nothing Sweeter in Life Than a Granddaughter*

*There Is So Much to Love About You... Daughter*

*Think Positive Thoughts Every Day*

*Words Every Woman Should Remember*

*You Are Stronger Than You Know*

# DREAM BIG, STAY POSITIVE,
## AND
# BELIEVE IN YOURSELF

Edited by Becky McKay

**Blue Mountain Press**™
Boulder, Colorado

We wish to thank Susan Polis Schutz for permission to reprint the following poems that appear in this publication: "Live Your World of Dreams" and "You cannot listen to what others...." Copyright © 1983, 1986 by Stephen Schutz and Susan Polis Schutz. And for "This life is yours." Copyright © 1979 by Continental Publications. All rights reserved.

Library of Congress Control Number: 2017949061
ISBN: 978-1-68088-192-9

◪ and Blue Mountain Press are registered in U.S. Patent and Trademark Office.
Certain trademarks are used under license.

Acknowledgments appear on page 92.

Printed in China.
First Printing: 2017

♻ This book is printed on recycled paper.

This book is printed on paper that has been specially produced to be acid free (neutral pH) and contains no groundwood or unbleached pulp. It conforms with the requirements of the American National Standards Institute, Inc., so as to ensure that this book will last and be enjoyed by future generations.

# Blue Mountain Arts, Inc.
P.O. Box 4549, Boulder, Colorado 80306

# CONTENTS

# DREAM
# BIG

The journey to your dreams is one that no one else will travel and no one else can judge — it's a path where the challenges are great and the rewards even greater.

It's a journey where each experience will teach you something valuable and you can't get lost, for you already know the way by heart.

It's a journey that is universal yet uniquely personal, and profound yet astonishingly simple — where sometimes you will stumble and other times you will soar.

You may not always know exactly where you're headed, but if you follow the desires of your heart, the integrity of your conscience, and the wisdom of your soul... then each step you take will lead you to discover more of who you really are, and it will be a step in the right direction on the journey to your dreams.

— Paula Finn

The dreams in your heart
are waiting to come true.
Give them wings —
and be all that you
could hope to be.

You can accomplish
more than you've ever imagined —
    as long as you believe.

There's no end
to the amazing things
    you can achieve —
if you set your mind to it.

Make a plan, and then —
one step at a time —
take the actions
that will bring your dreams to life.

Create the life
that you have always wished for —
because that is the life
you deserve.

Follow your dreams!

— Jason Blume

# FIND YOUR
# PASSION

Without passion, it's too difficult to persist when times
are hard and solutions are elusive. Without passion,
it's too difficult to remind yourself of the importance
of your journey when others doubt or criticize you.
Without passion, you won't be able to screen out the
noisy disturbances that undo less committed individuals.
Without passion, it's too hard to connect with others
about the importance of your mission and convince
them to help you and get on board. Without passion,
it's just another workmanlike goal, and not necessarily
the mission that will change your life — or the world.

———

Caroline Adams Miller

Passion is letting nothing
stand in the way of getting there.
Passion is the fire inside your spirit,
the force that propels you forward,
and the determination
to make your dreams real.
Passion is the voice inside you
that says "Go for it!"

Vickie M. Worsham

Passion is a critical element for anyone who wants to achieve a dream. Why? Because it is the starting point of all achievement. I have never seen anyone anywhere at any time achieve anything of any value without the spark of passionate desire! It provides the energy that makes dreams possible.

John C. Maxwell

# WHEN YOU NEED INSPIRATION, ASK YOURSELF...

1. If money were no object, what would I do all day?

2. If I could be anyone for a week, who would it be?

3. What conversation topic can I get lost in for hours?

4. If I walk into a bookstore, which section am I drawn to?

5. Who do I love to spend time with and why?

6. If you asked my partner/mother/best friend what I'm best at doing, what would they say?

7. Who was I as a kid?

8. What do people come to me for?

9. What do I feel least insecure about?

10. What's pure and simple fun for me?

11. If I had to write a book, what would it be about?

There is nothing more important than becoming who you are here to be. With the distractions of daily life, we often do not take time to look within and understand who it is that we really are. The time and courage taken to give life to the real you is your only true obligation to yourself.

When we live an inspired life, we live a joyful life. It is impossible not to. When we become who we really are, our life can transform, and the results are often bigger than we imagine, bigger than us. We have more confidence. We create more abundance. Our connection to the world is solidified. And the legacy, the ripple effect of us living a life we love, has an endless contribution on the lives of others. What is more important than that?

———

Susie Moore

# BE A DREAMER AND A DOER

Dreamers whose dreams come true
   are achievers.
They determine what it will take,
   and they resolve to do it.
They establish reasonable goals,
   and they meet them.
They set high expectations,
   and they strive for them.

Dreamers whose dreams come true
   are believers.
They see their dreams clearly.
They have faith that they can make
   them happen.
Their emotions, efforts, and actions
come from their desire and belief
that today's dreams are
   tomorrow's realities.

———

Barbara Cage

If one advances confidently in the direction of his dreams, and endeavors to live the life which he has imagined, he will meet with a success unexpected in common hours.

Henry David Thoreau

The world needs dreamers and the world needs doers. But above all, the world needs dreamers who do. Don't just entrust your hopes and wishes to the stars. Today, begin learning the craft that will enable you to reach for them.

Sarah Ban Breathnach

# SET GOALS...
## AND WORK HARD TO SEE THEM THROUGH

I recommend adopting two concurrent goals:

1. A long-term dream: It doesn't have to be realistic or even specific. For example, you might say you want to work in a specific field, travel the world, have more free time. Even a vague goal can provide direction.

2. An 18-month plan: Set personal goals for what you want to learn in the next year and a half. Ask yourself how you can improve and what you're afraid to do (that's usually the thing you should try).

Sheryl Sandberg

It's important to set goals and work hard no matter how many people tell you it's useless and you won't succeed. Without determination, your dreams of a better life won't come true.

Jackie Joyner-Kersee

Define success and define your best years by every day that you work hard toward achieving your goals. Your talent and efforts got you here today, and that talent will continue to open doors for you. And luck will play its part too. But a strong work ethic is vital, and it will get you farther than talent and luck ever could.

Octavia Spencer

# THINK OUTSIDE
# THE BOX

There is an old IQ test [that] was nine dots, and you had to draw five lines with the pencil within the nine dots without lifting the pencil.

The only way to do it was to go outside the box. So don't be afraid to go outside the box. Don't be afraid to think outside the box. Don't be afraid to fail big, to dream big.

———

Denzel Washington

Don't put limits on yourself.
So many dreams are waiting to be realized.
Decisions are too important to leave to chance.
Reach for your peak, your goal, your prize.

Realize that it's never too late.
Do ordinary things in an extraordinary way.
Have health and hope and happiness.
Take the time to wish upon a star.

— Collin McCarty

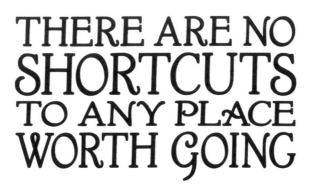

# THERE ARE NO SHORTCUTS TO ANY PLACE WORTH GOING

If you focus on making one small change at a time, eventually those small changes will add up to one big transformation. Don't wait for the "perfect moment" to appear or when everything is "just right."

It takes a leap of faith and some trust in the process to plant the seeds that will grow into a rewarding future. It takes courage to pursue your dreams and goals. Embrace the fear — it's only natural to be a little scared. It's a sign that you are ready to grow into the next chapter of your life.

Now is the time for you to become the person you have always dreamed of becoming… now is the perfect time to make your dreams come true.

Eileen Rosenfeld

# AIM HIGH

Dream lofty dreams,
and as you dream,
so shall you become.

———

John Ruskin

They build too low who build beneath the skies.

———

Edward Young

Imagine... Here you are, on the high peak of a mountain. You can choose to wing your way toward the clouds, or you can simply walk the usual, ordinary paths that lead to the valley below.

Which choice will you make — the well-worn paths or rising above it all?

Beautiful things await you if you can reach the heights.

———

George Sand

# DON'T LET YOUR DREAMS PASS YOU BY

There comes a time in your life when you realize that if you stand still, you will remain at this point forever. You realize that if you fall and stay down, life will pass you by.

Rather than wondering about or questioning the direction your life has taken, accept the fact that there is a path before you now. Shake off the "whys" and "what ifs," and rid yourself of confusion. Whatever was — is in the past. Whatever is — is what's important. The past is a brief reflection. The future is yet to be realized. Today is here. Cast your dreams to the stars.

Vicki Silvers

Let nothing hold you back from exploring
  your wildest fantasies, wishes, and
     aspirations.
Don't be afraid to follow your dreams
  wherever they lead you.
Open your eyes to their beauty;
open your mind to their magic;
open your heart to their possibilities.
Don't be afraid to take risks,
  to become involved,
     to make a commitment.
Only by dreaming will you ever discover
who you are, what you want,
  and what you can do.

Julie Anne Ford

# FOLLOW YOUR
# HEART

Go where the heart
longs to go
Don't pay attention to the feet
that want to stay rooted

Go where the mind
wants to explore
Don't worry about the hands
that still want to hold on

Go where your gut
is fearful to go
Don't let your body
sit in one place

Go where your heart
knows it should go

———

Natasha Josefowitz

Dreams guide us as we reach for the stars, follow our heart's desire, and do the things we are passionate about. Dreams help weave the fabric of who we are, and they reveal what matters most to us. They allow our spirits to shine, and they reflect our uniqueness and authenticity....

Dreaming is the way we define what matters to us and what we wish to accomplish and do in the world with this one life.

Sandra Magsamen

Let your dreams take you...
to the corners of your smiles,
to the highest of your hopes,
to the windows of your
opportunities,
and to the
most special places
your heart
has ever known.

———

Carson Wrenn

# JUST
# START!

Start by making a small promise to yourself; continue fulfilling that promise until you have a sense that you have a little more control over yourself. Now take the next level of challenge. Make yourself a promise and keep it until you have established control at that level. Now move to the next level; make a promise; keep it. As you do this, your sense of personal worth will increase; your sense of self-mastery will grow, as will your confidence that you can master the next level.

———

Stephen R. Covey

Begin where you are; work where you are;
the hour which you are now wasting, dreaming
of some far off success, may be crowded with
grand possibilities.

———

Orison Swett Marden

Whatever you vividly imagine, ardently desire,
sincerely believe, and enthusiastically act upon...
must inevitably come to pass.

———

Paul J. Meyer

# LIVE YOUR WORLD OF DREAMS

Lean against a tree
and dream your world of dreams
Work hard at what you like to do
and try to overcome all obstacles
Laugh at your mistakes
and praise yourself for learning from them

Pick some flowers
and appreciate the beauty of nature
Be honest with people
and enjoy the good in them
Don't be afraid to show your emotions
Laughing and crying make you feel better
Love your friends and family
    with your entire being
They are the most important part of your life
Feel the calmness on a quiet sunny day
and plan what you want to accomplish in life
Find a rainbow
and live your
world of dreams

Susan Polis Schutz

# STAY
## POSITIVE

The way you think shapes your world.
A positive attitude can open
the door to limitless possibilities.
When you give yourself
the freedom to dream and imagine,
your world expands.
The impossible becomes possible.
So breathe in peace and hope,
and give your dreams a chance.
Remember, transformation
is not only possible,
it happens every day;
think of butterflies, seeds,
and springtime.

Our world is full of new beginnings.
It is larger than any of us can comprehend.
Take heart, believe in big skies
and wide-open spaces,
and hold on to the promise
of mysteries and magic.
There is space for your dreams to grow.
The future may astonish you.

———————

Rebecca Brown

Life can make choices for us.
Sometimes these choices
    seem unhappy or unfair,
but in the end we control
our own destiny because we can decide
    how people and events affect us.

So much of our happiness lies within
    the choices we make.
We can accept that life
    isn't the way we want it to be,
    or we can change it so that it will be.
We can walk through the shadows,
    or we can choose to smile
    and seek out the sunlight.

We can create grand dreams
    that never leave the ground,
    or we can be builders of dreams that come true.
We can look at only the negative aspects of ourselves,
    or we can lift ourselves up
    by being our own best friend.
We can live in the past
    or dream about the future,
    or we can live for today.
We can give up when the road becomes difficult,
    or we can keep on going
    until the view is much better.
The choices in life are endless,
    and so is the potential for happiness.

Nancye Sims

# CELEBRATE
## YOUR SUCCESSES

Celebrate who you are,
because you would not have made it
to today by being just anybody.

Every time you won a fight with bravery
or lost a fight with grace,
every time you turned
mistakes to knowledge
and knowledge to action,
every time you painted the world brighter
with your talents
or unlocked new ideas with your words...
all those moments have made you
who you are right now —
someone who smiles at a challenge
and lives with a passion for the day.

Just as small drops of water
make up great oceans,
the small pieces of you
have created your great success.

---

Chrissy Tustison

$S$ustaining your mental fortitude and tenacity during a long and arduous process is difficult. Celebrating and leveraging all the things you do well and all of the successes along the way is the key to your success.

———

Denise Hill

$T$ake pride in your accomplishments as they are steppingstones to your dreams.

———

Shannon M. Lester

# BE WILLING
# TO FAIL

You've probably heard the expression, "Failure is not an option." Oh, really? Well, here's a reality check: failure had *better* be an option, because whether or not you consider it an option, it's going to happen! If you go through life with the philosophy that "failure is not an option," then you'll never have any good opportunities to learn.

If Babe Ruth had lived by the philosophy that *failure is not an option*, then you and I would have never heard of him. Why? Because Babe Ruth not only set a world record for home runs, he also led the league in strikeouts.

Jeff Olson

We all fail, backslide, and lose ground when trying to achieve something great. It is a part of the process. Instead of fixating on your failures, learn from them and hone in on your successes. Learn to forgive yourself, pick yourself up, and keep moving forward. So, you ate three donuts for breakfast, woke up late, and missed your gym session or failed a test. That one incident does not determine your success — regroup and keep it moving.

Denise Hill

Don't be discouraged by a failure. It can be a positive experience. Failure is, in a sense, the highway to success, inasmuch as every discovery of what is false leads us to seek earnestly after what is true.

John Keats

When the challenges seem so much greater than your strength, look back to past trials and tribulations that you have gone through and survived. The same strength that enabled you to get through those earlier storms is still within you. Reach down deep and draw from this wellspring; allow it to replenish your soul.

Borrow strength from others — those "warriors" who have already fought and won the battles you are struggling with today. Rejoice in their victories; they are with you in spirit. Draw strength from those who are with you in the battle today, for none of us truly walk alone.

Draw strength from the good things in your life —
from the simplest to the greatest. Whether it's a
pretty little flower, a kind word from a friend, a walk
in your favorite place, or a beautiful sunset — draw
strength from anything good that touches your heart
or your day.

Draw strength from those who love you — those
who make your life richer by being a part of your
days, those who will be there for you not only on
sunny days but also on the cloudy ones, and those
who will hold you in the storms of life.

Have faith in yourself. Draw strength from your
faith. And know in your heart that you have strength
for today.

———————

Nancye Sims

# HOLD YOUR HEAD HIGH

Go forward with your shoulders back, with your head high, and with a smile. With your enthusiastic spirit, perseverance, and integrity of character, put your intelligence, talents, and passion into action.

Never let setbacks excuse you from trying again. It often takes many attempts to be a success.

Never let negative people influence you or direct what you do. Always face forward and see your whole life shining bright for you. Never let go of your character, ideals, or activism for the good of this world.

Never let go of the passions that inspire you, guide you, and always smile on you. These passions will lead you to reach your fullest potential. Hold on to them, and they will keep you honest, caring, kind, and generous with the finest gifts your heart can give.

Jacqueline Schiff

# FACE
## YOUR FEARS

To understand why fear is good, one has to
stop viewing fear as a feeling, emotion, or
behavioral command and start looking at it
simply as information. Fear is good because
it is our brain's way of identifying the things
about which we are ignorant. Knowing this,
we should look at our fear not as a reason
to avoid the things that frighten us but as a
reason to engage them....

So don't be afraid of fear. Because it sharpens
you, it challenges you, it makes you stronger;
and when you run away from fear, you also
run away from the opportunity to be your
best possible self.

Ed Helms

I have learned to ask myself this: honestly, what is the worst that could happen?

When I have figured that out, I also spend a bit of time on trying to figure out what I could do if that often pretty unlikely thing happens.

I have over the years discovered that the worst thing that could realistically happen is usually not as scary as the nightmare my fear-fueled mind could produce.

Finding clarity in this way doesn't take much time or effort, and it can help you to avoid much mind-made suffering. And help you to get going, step outside of your comfort zone and take that chance.

Henrik Edberg

# REMEMBER WHAT IS MOST IMPORTANT...

It's not having everything go right;
it's facing whatever goes wrong.
It's not being without fear;
it's having the determination
    to go on in spite of it.
It's not where you stand,
but the direction you're going in.
It's more than never having bad moments;
it's knowing you are always
    bigger than the moment.
It's believing you have already
    been given everything you need
        to handle life.

It's not being able to rid
    the world of all its injustices;
it's being able to rise above them.
It's the belief in your heart
    that there will always be
more good than bad in the world.

Remember to live just this one day
and not add tomorrow's troubles
    to today's load.
Remember that every day ends
and brings a new tomorrow
full of exciting new things.

Vickie M. Worsham

# ENJOY THE JOURNEY

**W**hatever your goal in life, try to do it to the best of your ability but stay happy. Wherever you set your sights, don't get discouraged, and be proud of every day that you are able to work in that direction. Most of all, along the way, don't forget to stop and smell the roses.

———

Chris Evert

I would say to make sure you always have fun [with what you're doing], and to make sure that it's your decision. If it's not your decision, you're not having fun, and if you're not having fun, you might not enjoy it. If you're having fun, that's when the best memories are built.

———————

Simone Biles

The secret joys of living are not found by rushing from point A to point B, but by inventing some imaginary letters along the way.

———————

Douglas Pagels

Life doesn't always happen the way you want it to or the way you planned it or hoped for. Detours suddenly appear; storms blow in unexpectedly. The road you're traveling — that seemed so safe and secure — changes direction without warning, and life becomes something that's not at all what you thought it would be. You find there's nothing to do but stop for a while, figure out your options, and think about new decisions you have to make.

Life is forever changing. You can't always control what happens, but you can hang tough through it all and make the changes and decisions that are so necessary and will help you grow in spite of the disappointments, develop courage in spite of the adversities, be creative and come up with solutions, and always keep love in your heart.

No matter how hard things may seem... life will change again, and it's possible that this detour will lead you to a place that will bring you more happiness and let you reach more satisfying places in your heart and life than you've ever reached before.

Donna Levine-Small

# NEVER GIVE UP

Relentless...

Steady and persistent. Constant. Unyielding. Showing no signs of letup, no drop-off in intensity, severity, strength...

There's something very *Beyoncé* about the word, don't you think? It's empowering — so much so that I've taken to writing it on my wrist before I compete. It's engraved on a silver ring I like to wear. I've even got it printed on the band of my favorite pair of goggles.

*Relentless...*

It reminds me to keep on, moving ever forward, hard.... It tells me to reach deep down for my very best, even when it feels like there's nothing left. Even when every muscle in my body is telling me I'm done.

Missy Franklin

People who fulfill their dreams are not merely lucky; neither are they necessarily the most talented. Rather, they understand the value of perseverance and determination. They believe that setbacks are simply a means to grow, and that small failures only pave the way for new insights. They know where they are going even when others do not and believe in their own dreams when others doubt. Their vision comes from within — and it is always burning in their hearts.

Lisa Crofton

Don't ever try to understand everything —
some things will just never make sense.
Don't ever be reluctant
    to show your feelings —
    when you're happy, give in to it!
    When you're not, live with it.
Don't ever be afraid to try to
    make things better —
    you might be surprised at the results.
Don't ever take the weight of the world
    on your shoulders.

Don't ever feel threatened by the future —
    take life one day at a time.
Don't ever feel guilty about the past —
    what's done is done. Learn from any
    mistakes you might have made.
Don't ever feel that you are alone —
    there is always somebody there for you
    to reach out to.
Don't ever forget that you can achieve
    so many of the things you can imagine —
    imagine that! It's not as hard as it seems.
Don't ever stop loving,
    don't ever stop believing,
        don't ever stop dreaming your dreams.

Laine Parsons

# LOOK
## TO THE
# FUTURE

Having a clear vision of what you desire evokes a sense of excitement and issues an invitation to the future to pull you forward. Believing in your vision is the surest way to attract what you want in life; the key is to keep that vision energized with positive thoughts for tomorrow, regardless of what today looks like.

———

Iyanla Vanzant

Anxiety and depression can fuel procrastination because it's easier to give up when unhappiness rules our thinking. One of the best ways to deal with this is to "time travel" and imagine an important goal has been reached — instead of focusing only on the work in front of you.... The positive emotions generated by imagining a completed goal can lift a person's mood and allow them to get started on, or stick with, hard work.

Caroline Adams Miller

# TOMORROW IS WHERE DREAMS COME TRUE

Don't spend too much time looking in the rearview mirror. <u>Yesterday</u> is behind you. What's done is done, and it's important to take what you've learned from the experience and just move on.

Today is a brand-new opportunity, a blank canvas, an unwritten page in the diary. All that needs to happen right now is for you... to do the amazing things you're capable of.

And tomorrow? That's the place where dreams come true. You'll need to be smart and stay strong to live the life you want to have. But don't ever forget: you are creative and capable and wise, and you have what it takes to make your days everything you want them to be.

———

Douglas Pagels

# BELIEVE IN
# YOURSELF

Look in the mirror
and see what others see —
a talented, uplifting,
and magnificent person
who can do anything
and everything.

Believe in your heart
that you have the power
to grab hold of your future
and mold it into the things
you have always dreamed of.

Trust in your soul
that you are capable of doing
all that needs to be done.

Know that you are
incredible in every way
and see yourself
as others see you...
as intelligent
and spectacular.

Lamisha Serf-Walls

You've got a brilliance inside you
that outshines any star.
Never forget who you are,
what you stand for,
or what you've been through before.
All these things
will strengthen your spirit
and help you out
as you make your way
into new adventures
and stand up to adversities.

There is nothing that
you can't overcome
with strength of heart
and a little bit of courage.
You are a unique
and talented individual
who has everything it takes
to succeed in this life.

―――――――

Ashley Rice

# BE TRUE
## TO THE LIGHT
## WITHIN YOU

We do carry an inner light, an inner compass, and the reason we don't know we carry it is because we've been distracted. We think that the light is actually being carried by a leader or somebody that we have elected or somebody that we very much admire, and that that's the only light. So we forget that we have our own light — it may be small, it may be flickering, but it's actually there. So what we need to do, I think, is to be still enough to let that light shine and illuminate our inner landscape and our dreams — especially our dreams. And then our dreams will lead us to the right way.

Alice Walker

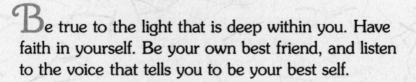

Be true to the light that is deep within you. Have faith in yourself. Be your own best friend, and listen to the voice that tells you to be your best self.

Be true to yourself in the paths that you choose. Follow your talents and passions; don't take the roads others say you must follow because they are the most popular. Take the paths where your talents will thrive — the ones that will keep your spirits alive with enthusiasm and everlasting joy. Follow your inner light.

———————

Jacqueline Schiff

Somewhere inside you —
where the joy of life resides,
where beliefs are planted, and
where magic lives — there's a
wish waiting to come true.
Go there now and see it in
full bloom.

Somewhere inside you...
there's a part of you that
counts your hours by the
happy moments, not all the
things you haven't done...

It's where you keep your
favorite memories — and
regrets are not allowed.
It's that place in you that's
infinite and limitless and
always without boundaries —
and where you embrace every
dream with all your heart.

Donna Fargo

We can do whatever we wish to do provided
our wish is strong enough.

Katherine Mansfield

# YOU GET TO
# DECIDE

The best years are very much ahead of you. And they can be whatever you want them to be. Your work, your life, your weekdays, your weekends, can all be filled with as much meaning as you dictate.

———

Octavia Spencer

How will you use your gifts? What choices will you make?

Will inertia be your guide, or will you follow your passions?

Will you follow dogma, or will you be original?

Will you choose a life of ease, or a life of service and adventure?

Will you wilt under criticism, or will you follow your convictions?

Will you bluff it out when you're wrong, or will you apologize?

Will you guard your heart against rejection, or will you act when you fall in love?

Will you play it safe, or will you be a little bit swashbuckling?

When it's tough, will you give up, or will you be relentless?

Will you be a cynic, or will you be a builder?

Will you be clever at the expense of others, or will you be kind?

———————

Jeff Bezos

# KNOW YOUR OWN WORTH

You have so much to offer,
     so much to give, and
     so much you deserve
     to receive in return.
Don't ever doubt that.

Know yourself and all of your fine
     qualities.
Rejoice in all your marvelous strengths
     of mind and body.

Be glad for the virtues that are yours,
    and pat yourself on the back for all
    your many admirable achievements.
Keep positive.
Concentrate on that which makes you happy,
    and build yourself up.
Stay nimble of heart,
    happy of thought,
    healthy of mind, and
    well in being.

———

Janet A. Sullivan-Bradford

# TAKE THE
# LEAP

When you believe in yourself, it fuels your creativity, your ambitions, and your motivation to do things. It also helps you to take a leap of faith when it comes to going after what it is that you truly desire.

All successful people from Gandhi to Tesla believed in themselves. They also believed in their vision, and this is what gave them the drive to succeed and carry through with their goals....

We all have to trust that we are capable and have the ability to turn the impossible into the possible.

When you truly believe in yourself and your abilities, success will always follow, no matter what you are looking to achieve.

Tanaaz Chubb

When you come to believe
in all that you are
and all that you can become,
there will be no cause for doubt.
Believe in your heart,
for it offers hope.
Believe in your mind,
for it offers direction.
Believe in your soul,
for it offers strength.
But above all else...
believe in yourself.

———

Leslie Neilson

# IGNORE THE NAYSAYERS

It's no secret that throughout life, people will always try to sell you on shortcuts and the easy way out, and they will tell you what you cannot do. There will always be naysayers. There will always be people telling you that the timing just isn't quite right, that the work just isn't important, and that the world just isn't ready. You know what we have to do? Prove them wrong!

Debbie Wasserman Schultz

You cannot listen
to what others
want you to do
You must listen
to yourself
Society
family
friends
and loved ones
do not know what
you must do
Only you know
and only you
can do what is
right for you

Susan Polis Schutz

# DREAM THE IMPOSSIBLE

All who have accomplished
   great things
have had a great aim
and fixed their gaze
on a goal which was high —
one which sometimes seemed
   impossible.

———

Orison Swett Marden

Some men see things
as they are and say, why?

I dream of things that
never were and say, why not?

George Bernard Shaw

The future belongs to those who believe
in the beauty of their dreams.

Author Unknown

Nothing is impossible to a willing heart.

John Heywood

# YOU HAVE THE POWER TO MAKE YOUR DREAMS COME TRUE

This life is yours
Take the power
to choose what you want to do
and do it well
Take the power
to love what you want in life
and love it honestly

Take the power
to walk in the forest
and be a part of nature
Take the power
to control your own life
No one else can do it for you
Take the power
to make your life
healthy
exciting
worthwhile
and very happy

Susan Polis Schutz

Today is your greatest opportunity — seize it! Don't look back and wish you had done more yesterday; don't look ahead and get overwhelmed by what may lie there. Do the best you can in this moment with the tools you have at hand. Know that each step you take, no matter how small it may seem now, will, over time, add up to a tremendous journey of discovery on your way to achieving whatever you dream of doing.

———

Avery Jakobs

Life is a blank page,
an open highway,
a ticket with your name on it.
Life is a friend and a dream
and a pencil in your hand.
Life is where the day takes you
and what you've got
in your back pocket.

Life is kicking back over coffee,
talking about where
we have been,
walking along on the same road.
Life is a long story
and a song that continues.
Life is all this.
Life is today.

———————

Ashley Rice

# GO
## ALL IN!

Bet on yourself because you deserve it. It is risky to get uncomfortable and decide to be the maker of your own fate. But who else do you trust more than yourself? Nobody else can do it for you. You will even surprise yourself along the journey once you let go and just go all in!

Get out of your own way with fear, doubt, and negativity. Instead imagine the possibilities and be confident in your ability to win! It would be a shame to always think about the "what-ifs." Nope, you're better than that!

So, what are you waiting for? Don't prolong your success any longer. Take the chance and bet on yourself!

Sarah Danielle

Believe Big. Adjust your thermostat forward. Launch your success offensive with honest, sincere belief that you can succeed. Believe big and grow big.

David J. Schwartz, PhD

Have the daring to accept yourself as a bundle of possibilities and undertake the game of making the most of your best.

Henry Emerson Fosdick

Believe in everything
you set out to do.
Believe in yourself
right down to your shoes.

Believe in wishes made
on falling stars
and whispered into fountains.

Fall in love with your dreams.
Keep them with you every day.
Let them grow to be
bigger than the sun.

You have magic inside you —
imagination,
heart,
and soul.
Believe in yourself,
believe in your dreams,
and you can go anywhere
and you can do anything.

———————

Charley Knox

# YOU ARE MEANT FOR MEANT FOR GREAT THINGS

Because each day can be
better than the last...
Because miracles surround us
everywhere we go...
Because dreams are worth fighting for
with everything we've got...

Because life is too short
to hold grudges
or to ever look back...
Because some things
are worth waiting for...
Live your life to the fullest every day,
in every possible way.
You are meant for great things,
and you will never regret
pursuing your dreams!

—————

Ashley Rice

# DREAM BIG, STAY POSITIVE,

### AND

# BELIEVE IN YOURSELF

If a star twinkles… wish on it. When you spot a rainbow… search for the gold. Walk on the sunny side; dream on a cloud. Always remember that life is meant to be enjoyed. Fill your life with wonder and your days with beauty. Set your dreams on the farthest star.

When you're caught between a rock and a hard place… plant a seed. Chart your course; map out your future. Sail away on your own cruise line, and remember there's no limit to how far you can go.

Believe in miracles. Look for silver linings. When the going gets tough… let faith smooth the way. Dreams come in all shapes and sizes. Do the things that warm your soul. Inspire yourself. Make good things happen. In every tomorrow a new promise shines.

Believe in yourself. Honor your strengths. A little hope and determination can overcome anything. Life is a candle… and you're its spark. Soar high and far. Open your arms and let life's good things come in.

Live your wishes. Blaze your own trail straight to the stars.

———

Linda E. Knight

# ACKNOWLEDGMENTS

We gratefully acknowledge the permission granted by the following authors, publishers, and authors' representatives to reprint poems or excerpts from their publications:

Paula Finn for "The journey to your dreams…." Copyright © 2013 by Paula Finn. All rights reserved.

Jason Blume for "The dreams in your heart…." Copyright © 2015 by Jason Blume. All rights reserved.

Sounds True for "Without passion, it's too difficult…" and "Anxiety and depression can fuel…" from *Getting Grit: The Evidence-Based Approach to Cultivating Passion, Perseverance, and Purpose* by Caroline Adams Miller. Copyright © 2017 by Caroline Adams Miller. All rights reserved.

Vickie M. Worsham for "Passion is letting nothing…." Copyright © 2017 by Vickie M. Worsham. All rights reserved.

Thomas Nelson, Inc., www.thomasnelson.com, for "Passion is a critical element…" from *Put Your Dream to the Test* by John C. Maxwell. Copyright © 2009, 2011 by John C. Maxwell. All rights reserved.

Susie Moore and *Greatist* for "If money were no object…" from "The 11 Questions to Ask Yourself When You Feel Uninspired," *Greatist* (blog), July 19, 2016, https://greatist.com/live/motivation-tips-questions-to-ask-to-get-inspired. Copyright © 2016 by Susie Moore. All rights reserved.

Barbara Cage for "Dreamers whose dreams come true…." Copyright © 2017 by Barbara Cage. All rights reserved.

Hachette Book Group for "The world needs dreamers…" from *Simple Abundance* by Sarah Ban Breathnach. Copyright © 1995 by Sarah Ban Breathnach. All rights reserved. And for "It's important to set goals…" from *A Kind of Grace* by Jackie Joyner-Kersee with Sonja Steptoe. Copyright © 1997 by Jackie Joyner-Kersee. All rights reserved.

Sheryl Sandberg for "I recommend adopting two concurrent goals" from "Session with Sheryl Sandberg," *Quora* (blog), December 15, 2015, https://www.quora.com/What-would-Sheryl-Sandberg-tell-her-younger-self-when-starting-out. Copyright © 2015 by Sheryl Sandberg. All rights reserved.

Octavia Spencer for "Define success and define your best years…" and "The best years are very much…" (commencement speech), Kent State University, May 14, 2017. Copyright © 2017 by Octavia Spencer. All rights reserved.

Denzel Washington for "There is an old IQ test…" from "Fall Forward" (commencement speech), Dillard University, May 7, 2015. Copyright © 2015 by Denzel Washington. All rights reserved.

Eileen Rosenfeld for "There Are No Shortcuts to Any Place Worth Going." Copyright © 2017 by Eileen Rosenfeld. All rights reserved.

Natasha Josefowitz for "Go where the heart longs to go." Copyright © 1996 by Natasha Josefowitz. All rights reserved.

Sandra Magsamen for "Dreams guide us as we reach…" from "Dream It, Believe It, Be It," *Oprah*, September 11, 2009, http://www.oprah.com/spirit/dream-it-believe-it-be-it. Copyright © 2009 by Sandra Magsamen. All rights reserved.

Franklin Covey Co. for "Start by making a small promise…" from *Principle-Centered Leadership* by Stephen R. Covey. Copyright © 1992 by Stephen R. Covey. All rights reserved.

The Leading Edge Publishing Company for "Whatever you vividly imagine…" by Paul J. Meyer. Copyright © 1997 by Paul J. Meyer. All rights reserved.

Denise Hill for "Sustaining your mental fortitude…" and "We all fail, backslide, and…" from "How to Stay Motivated Even Though You Can't See Yourself Moving Forward," *Lifehack*, June 21, 2017, http://www.lifehack.org/606200/motivation-move-forward?ref=category_section_post_17853. Copyright © 2017 by Denise Hill. All rights reserved.